To:_____

From:_____

Wolf Ways

A Story of the Wolf Family

Created by Leyton Jay Cougar
Written by Georgia H. Garner - Cougar and Leyton Jay Cougar
illustrated by:
J. Evans
Quirsten Ray Flores
and Leyton J. Cougar

Wolf Ways

A Story of the Wolf Family

Dedicated to: Sylvia...

Wolf families sing in their own special way.
All howling together to greet the new day.
Excited to see what the day will bring.
Wolves love to be free and wolves love to sing.

Boy wolf meets girl wolf, love at first sight.
They hunt and play by day, sleep together at night.
Throughout the days they care for each other.
Soon the young female will become a mother.

Father and mother search all around,
until the right place for a den is found.

Mother works hard to dig her den.

A safe and warm place to have puppies in.

As mother wolf yawns,
she shows us her teeth.
Twenty on top,
twenty-two beneath.
Running for miles, she's a
good hunter too.
But she has a new job when
her babies are due.

She's made a safe home she dug in the ground.
When her pups are born, they weigh just one pound.
Snug in their den mother and pups stay.
With mother's rich milk, they grow stronger each day.

Some of the pack joins together to run.
They are searching for food not just having fun.
To survive in the woods, wolves form a family group, mother and father wolf are the leaders of this troupe.

His nose to the ground father
wolf picks up the scent.
His prey is deer, and he knows
where they went.
Swiftly he runs ahead
of the bunch,
they are quiet and quick to
capture their lunch.

Father wolf has hunted and brings home some meat.
He stops by the den so that mother can eat.
Working together until pups are grown.
Proud parents make sure pups are never alone.

Here is father wolf with his bright yellow eyes.
Next to mother wolf he's larger in size.
Grey and brown fur keeps him warm when it's cold.
When hunting for food he is smart, fast and bold.

Soon mother and pups are outside in the sun. Quickly the pups will be looking for fun. Pups watch their parents to learn how to be adult wolves in the woods with their own family.

At about five weeks old,
a pup may stray.
Mother brings him
back right away.
Back to the den she holds
him with care.
Puppy stays still until
they get there.

While mother and father hunt with the pack.

Auntie cares for pups 'til parents get back.
All of the pack does their share,
to help raise pups with their wise gentle care.

Young and carefree, pups romp and play.
Learning while playing is the most fun way.
Wolf pups run, wrestle, and practice their bite.
Not hurting each other, they only play fight.

Father is quick to teach
right from wrong.
They must behave so they all
get along.
He looks very angry, but
the pups all know.
He never will hurt them
though his teeth show.

Trying to see who can hold on longer.
Tug-of-war games help the pups grow stronger.

Wolf pups love games that help them grow.

Hoping to learn all that their parents know.

Father wolf teaches his pup how to sing.

Wolves have a song for most everything.

They call to each other from miles away, or sing just to celebrate all they discovered that day.

The pups are now older
and soon will be grown.
They will stay with the pack
or form packs
of their own.
Maybe someday they'll be
digging a den, and this
wolf puppy story
will start once again.

Gathering together at the end of the day.

Howling a song as the moon lights their way.

We've learned about wolves and it's easy to see,

wolves love to sing and wolves love to be free.

color me

www.ingramcontent.com/pod-product-compliance
Lightning Source LLC
Chambersburg PA
CBHW041653260326

41914CB00018B/1632